P9-DZM-168

A LITTLE BOOK OF ANIMAL RIDDLES

Jim Murphy

SCHOLASTIC INC.

New York Toronto London Auckland Sydney

To Barbara

No part of this publication may be reproduced in whole or in part, or stored in a retrieval system, or transmitted in any form or by any means, electronic, mechanical, photocopying, recording, or otherwise, without written permission of the publisher. For information regarding permission, write to Scholastic Inc., 730 Broadway, New York, NY 10003.

ISBN 0-590-41193-4

Copyright © 1988 by James Murphy.
All rights reserved. Published by Scholastic Inc.
Art direction by Diana Hrisinko
Book design by Theresa Fitzgerald

12 11 10 9 8 7 6 5 4 3 2 1 8 9/8 0 1 2 3/9

Printed in the U.S.A. 08
First Scholastic printing, March 1988

What does an elephant do when he breaks his toe?
He calls a tow truck.

Why do little pigs
eat so much?
They want to make hogs of themselves.

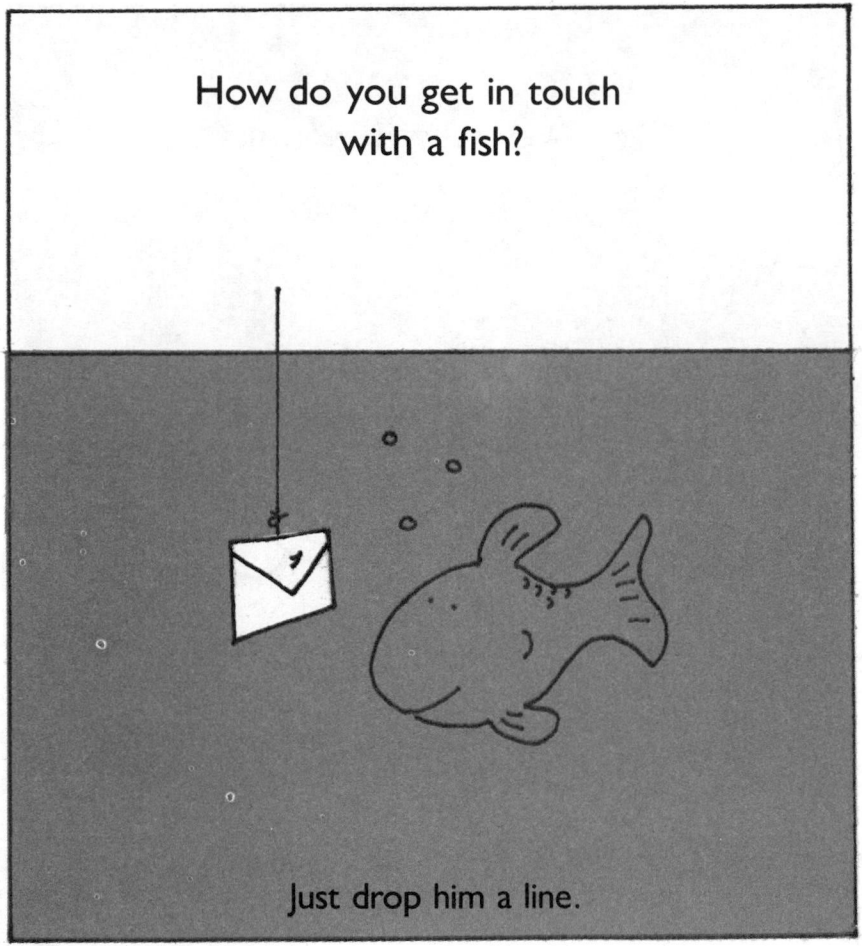
How do you get in touch with a fish?
Just drop him a line.

What happened when the monkey saw the banana?

The banana split.

What side of a chicken
has the most feathers?

The outside.

Why did the elephant run
away from the circus?

He was tired of working for peanuts.

Why don't little leopards like
to play hide and seek?

Because they are always spotted.

Why shouldn't you put an ad in the newspaper if your dog runs away?

Dogs can't read.

What do hippopotamuses have that no other animal has?

Baby Hippopotamuses.

Why is it hard to carry on a conversation with a goat around?

He keeps butting in.

What do they call little gray cats in California?

Kittens.

What is a twip?

A twip is what a wabbit takes
when he wides on a twain.

Why was the mother owl worried about her little son?

He just didn't give a hoot.

What do you call an
Eskimo cow?
An Eskimoo.

Why do hummingbirds hum?

They don't know the words.

How do you know when there is an elephant in your refrigerator?

You can't close the door.

Why don't giraffes eat very much?
They make a little go a long way.

Why do mother kangaroos
hate rainy days?

The kids have to play inside.

Why do cows wear bells?

Their horns don't work.

What is black and white and black and white and black and white?

A penguin rolling down a snowbank.

What is gray, has big ears and a trunk,
and weighs less than a pound?

A mouse going on vacation.

THE END